A Bullfrog
at Café du Monde

Photographs by
Christopher R. Harris

JULIA HOUSE PUBLISHING CO.
New Orleans

FIRST EDITION

JULIA HOUSE PUBLISHING CO.
P.O. Box 24224
New Orleans, Louisiana 70184

Cover Art by Julia Nead

ISBN 0-9614228-1-5

Printed in the United States of America

Acknowledgements

I would like to thank the caffeine muses of True Brew café; Barbara Harding, the good witch of words and wastebaskets; Gary Esolen, master poet and gentle teacher; and my wife Debby, who, for me, is the fertile earth of all good things.

Dedication

These poems are dedicated
to the people of New Orleans.

There will be no snow this Christmas
And a small mound called Monkey Hill
Is our city's highest spot —
But you can't have everything,
And this is what we got.

Preface

If you bring your own coffee when you leave town, if you believe the word "axe" is a verb, if you consider Halloween a major holiday, then these poems are for you.

If you are not familiar with New Orleans some of these poems may require a little work, but give it a try. After all, for generations deep south readers have cheerfully translated metaphor imported from the cold country. My hero Robert Frost sent us "frozen-ground-swells," a "cord of maple," and birches bent by "ice storms." If you find that you need a little help, ask a local, but be sure you have at least an hour to spare — you may find yourself sipping refreshment in the shaded courtyard of the Napoleon House as a friendly native explains the origin of the phrase "neutral ground."

Whoever you may be, visitor, native, friend or family, open your heart to our city and hear her declaration:

I am the Lady of the River
the city of your dreams
and I am stronger than I seem.
Stay with me.
Believe in me.
Love me.
I will be young again.

Uptown Downtown

We got four directions
to help you get around:
>*Uptown Downtown*
>*Riverside and Lake*

Once you know the secret
You won't make no mistake.

Now, South Carrollton and South Claiborne
They meet to form a cross,
So if you're thinking North and South
It's gonna get you lost.
And in the evening
When you cross the river
From the East Bank to the West,
And the sun is set behind your back
It can make your mind a mess!

So forget about your compass,
And listen one more time:
>*Uptown Downtown*
>*Riverside and Lake*

Once you learn the system
You won't make no mistake.

The City of New Orleans Blues

Sometimes I think about leaving,
And sometimes I wonder
If I'm not missing out,
If there ain't some other place
I oughta be.

That's when she browns onions
In an iron skillet
And sings to me,
With whiskey breath,
Her sad wailing song
About steamboats and chains
Making levees
Pounding rains
Driving piles to build a house
And flambeaux.

Then when I'm asleep in bed,
She hexes up the spirits of the river
To fill my head with the smell
Of black molasses…
And she hugs me,
With big sweaty arms
She holds me deep and strong,
and I hear myself murmur in the dark,

Lord, I don't know what's right or wrong,
But bury my bones above the ground
'Cuz on this river's where I belong —
Right here's where I belong.

A Bullfrog at Café du Monde

A waiter wipes the table
And sets down coffee
Black as a Haitian slave,
Mixed with scalded milk
To make it muddy as the river
That flows a hundred yards away.
And beignets,
Fried hot and sprinkled
With powdered sugar so thick
I hold my breath
To take a bite.

It starts to rain,
Steam rises knee-high
From the asphalt,
Artists scramble
And the Old Pontalba building
Wets to an earthen red,

I rock back in my chair,
My belly presses
Against the buttons of my shirt,
A contented groan
Swells in my chest
And startles the lady at the next table.
The waiter buzzes by,
I reach out,
Catch him by the elbow
And croak:
"More coffee, please."

The Brown Stream

You Americans
Have been puttin' stuff in our river
For twenty-three hundred miles.
Your cornfields drain in it,
Your factories drool in it,
And your cities…
I shudder now to think it,
'Cuz when it finally reaches us
We clean it up and drink it.

Monday at Mandina's
(With Apologies to Shelley's Ozymandias)

Ten thousand years from now
Some traveler from a modern land
Will come here to dig.
He'll find scattered mounds of powdered brick
Overgrown with wild azaleas
As he follows patches of a wide street
From an ancient burial ground
Toward where a river used to curl.
And somewhere half along the way
He'll find Mandina's,
And curious that it alone should stand
He'll come in,
And we'll all be there,
And we'll be eatin' red beans and rice,
'Cuz when everything else is gone
That'll be the only way to know
When it's Monday in Nu Awlins.

A Question to Our Founder

Jean Baptiste Le Moyne, Seur de Bienville

Almost three centuries ago
In the clear light of day
You came ashore
Cut away the canebrake
And named the space you cleared New
    Orleans.

And here we have lived ever since,
In this depression
Between river and lake,
Here in this watery home
To snakes and ducks and alligators,
Without benefit of webbed feet,
In this primeval puddle
We have survived.

Now I'd like to ask a question
And I'll try not to be provoking,
But when you picked this spot for us
What was it you were smoking?

All Saints' Day *(To "Ma B.")*

What do I do at the cemetery?
I get my bucket and broom
And I clean the family tomb.

It's nice,
I see old friends
And we talk about the people we remember.
I read the names on our tomb,
I figure out the ages
And wonder who'll be next,
But I really don't feel sad.

You can smell the stagnant water
So I wash the vase
And fill it fresh
With chrysanthemums
And something from our garden,
Something from home.
My grandmother used to bring
Branches from her bay tree,
She always brought bay leaves.

I arrange the flowers,
I step back and look,
Move this one a little,
Switch these two
And look again,
I arrange and rearrange,
But I can never get it perfect.
What else can you do?

I know they're not there —
Just their bones —
But I won't neglect them,
If they can see me
They know I don't neglect them.

Campaign Promises

Now we know you want
To campaign on the issues,
But we took a poll
And it's pretty clear
What the people want to hear.

You'll promise more policemen,
You'll cut the property tax,
You'll fix up all the potholes
And get government off our backs.

"Where will all the money come from?"
How the goody-goods will groan...
Well there's fat inside that budget
And you'll cut it to the bone.

You'll fire all the deadheads!
You'll eliminate the waste!
You'll restructure all the spending
On a zero budget base!

My boy, you can say almost anything
But avoid the cardinal sin:
As long as you don't tell the truth
I'm sure we're gonna win.

The Old Gentilly Highway

"Which road will we take today?"
He laughed
From behind the wheel
Of our '54 Plymouth.

"Take Snake Road!"
"No, Turtle Road!"
"No, Wild Man Road!"
We squealed from the back seat.

There was only one road
From New Orleans to Bay St. Louis,
But because that day
He decided to call it Turtle road,
We watched ahead,
As if on safari,
Determined to see turtles.

Hurricane

She's alone out there in the Gulf.
Her black clouds boil
Like spells in a witch's cauldron.
Wild as a cossack dancer
She whirls tornadoes in her wake.
She crawls,
Like a cosmic spider
She creeps,
She seeks land.

They say it will hit by morning
So I tape windows
Gather candles
And wait,
But there is no place to hide.
We have no inventions to tame
This atmospheric bulldozer
That pushes oceans in its path.

In the back yard
Something is wrong with the grass,
The green is not the same.
I have never breathed air like this before!
The pear tree,
Possessed,
Bends hard and shudders in a sudden gust
   of wind,
Wild wind
That rushes over me
So when I spread my arms
I'm flying.

And I hope it doesn't stop,
I hope she doesn't turn away...
Deep inside,
I hope she comes.

Gomorrah

Clouds close the sky,
The temperature falls,
It will rain today.

Like guardian angels,
The pumps stand motionless,
Massive
Smooth steel and oiled,
Polished shiny as the day
Our grandfathers cast them
A generation ago.

The rain begins.
It licks away the grime
Of a summer day,
Dives through iron grates into blackness,
Sloshes around corners
Surprising drainpipe creatures,
Gathers to a rage
And plunges into open canals.

There is a low electric hum.
A wheel, spoked with copper windings
Bigger than a man,
Begins to move.
With less vibration than an electric razor
A shaft the size of a tree trunk
Spins to a blur,
Pulls a river in,
And lifts it up and out
To lake level.

The sky clears,
The temperature rises,
And a city,
Five feet below sea level
And surrounded by water on all sides,
Is dry.
Knock on wood.

Mysterious Algiers

Ninth Ward born and raised,
He stood on the Moon Walk
And watched the ferry
Slide sideways across the river,
And suddenly
As when French children
First look across Gibraltar,
He saw it…

Algiers!

Good Eatin'

The sign read:
  CRAWFISH
  FROG LEGS
  TURTLE MEAT
  ALLIGATOR TAIL

And I thought
Damn!
There ain't *nothin'* safe
On Bayou LaFourche.

On a Hot October Morning

Humidity has drowned the muse.
This loaf of bread suggests nothing
It is good only for toast,
This coffee is just coffee,
And my soul,
Flat as stale rootbeer,
Grows mold.

But I perservere,
For as the days grow short
I know someday Autumn's got to come,
And when she does
She'll sprinkle metaphor
Like falling acorns.
This loaf of bread will glow:
    Yeast and stone-ground grain,
    a rising brotherhood
    in the oven of adversity.
The coffee:
    A baptismal rain
    to rinse life
    from these layers of roasted ash.

Yeah, she'll be here any day,
And my spirit is gonna prance fat
And gobble
Like a Thanksgiving turkey!
But for now,
Pass the butter —
I'm hungry.

Ghosts of N. Claiborne Avenue

There were trees here once,
Patron saints,
Three miles of double-rowed oaks,
That gathered in the sun
And made shade for us.

We celebrated Mardi Gras here.
Skeletons
With white bone faces,
Baby dolls
With rougey cheeks
And bare woman legs,
Indians
With sequins shining
And feathers spread like light from the sun.
A grazing herd,
We ate and laughed
And danced the greens all day.

I stand now in a forest of concrete pillars
Under eight lanes of elevated interstate.
My eyes draw down
To the great lifeless roots
Entombed beneath this slab,
Beneath this parking lot,
Buried forever.

Escape Velocity

When Ash Wednesday showed up
Like an old girlfriend
He packed his bag
Walked to Metairie Road
And tried to thumb a ride out of town.

But he kept looking back.
He thought about po'boys,
Barq's rootbeer,
Go-cups,
The natural feel of dancing in the street…
And he hardly felt the tug
As the Big Easy, like mother earth,
Pulled him in.

Now he eats King Cake in February,
Drinks Dixie longnecks in June
And wonders each August
How thirty-one days can take so long.
But who can blame him…
He tried to leave.

Ruthie the Duck Lady

What kind of creature
Could steal Ruthie's duck?
He orders Mile-High Pie
And watches it melt;
At a parade
He leaves doubloons on the ground
And won't yell "Throw me something,
    Mister!"
When he eats crawfish
He don't suck the heads...
And thus isolated from life's simple pleasures
He stalked the shadows of Decatur Street
And descended on poor Ruthie's duck.

When we found her in Jackson Square
And gave her another duck
She tucked it under her arm,
Sniffed
And floated toward the Cathedral on
    rollerskates.

Now everything is back to normal —
General Jackson is on his horse,
There are no cracks in the flood wall,
And Ruthie the Duck Lady is once again
    with duck.

Grinding Season *(To Ronnie)*

He crouched in a blind
With two of his sons
As the marsh awoke around him,
And gloried in the hunt of a lifetime.

There in the bow of his mudboat
He sipped his last cold beer,
Leaned forward,
Reached to splash water on his face,
And left us.

Today we held each other
And cried till evening.
Five brothers,
Six rocking chairs.
The cane stood tall in the field,
We felt the wind turn cold
And we knew that grinding season,
Like chimes on the hour,
Had just begun.

The Dew Poem

As I walked the levee this morning
I found a poem.
Some young poet had left it on the grass
To be forgotten in the dew.
As I read it to the birds
I felt his struggle
And wished I knew his name,
And wished that I could tell him
That the sky will turn gold in the evening,
And the river widens
As it runs to the open sea.

A New Orleans Trial Lawyer
At the Gates of Heaven

"You're a close case,"
 St. Peter said
 From behind the pearly gate,
"I'm not real sure.
 Sometimes you simply wouldn't listen
 And sometimes you were great.
 I just don't know."

Then with a twinkle in his eye
 and a voice that woke the angels
 So that a golden head
 Popped out from every cloud,
 Bob Zibilich cleared his throat and said,
"I see what you mean
 It really is a problem
 We can't pretend it's not
 But I wonder,
 Do you suppose we could gather up
 Perhaps a dozen souls
 From both sides of the gate,
 We'll tell them all the facts
 You your side
 Me mine
 And we'll let them decide.
 What do you think?"

Just then a voice filled the dome of heaven.
"PETER!
Don't do it!
If you give that man a jury,
Anything might happen.
He's done it before, you know —
Stood alone between heaven and hell
And changed the course of time.
He might set up his practice right here!
We'd be up to our necks in sinners,
He'd get 'em all in.
Look into his heart, Peter,
And stop wasting time.
Open the gate
And let him in."

The Times-Picayune

At four a.m. it wasn't here.
I heard a garbage truck
Grumble in the distance,
Stars arched overhead
In a preview of the coming season,
A single bird chirped,
but there was no paper.

I retreated to the kitchen
And in ritual anticipation
Boiled water for the coffee.

But now,
Just moments later
On this very patch of St. Augustine,
As if conjured here
By the rising sun,
As if whistled into time and space
By a flock of hungry birds,
Like manna in the desert,
Behold!
The Times-Picayune.

I whisk it up
And head for the kitchen
Confident,
For I, last of a chain of primeval survivors
I, first among the creatures of the earth,
I, child of the space age,
I may now begin my day.

River Revival

She'd loved them all,
Riverboat dandies,
Cotton money,
Loud-talking oil men.
They waltzed her from the Mississippi
Past the Parish line,
And when she reached for more
They built bridges to keep her ankles dry,
And no one could deny her
While she was a star.

But there were so many years,
She used more make-up.
Curtsied for tourists,
And took in boarders
Till the blood lay like tar in her veins
And she crawled old and aching
Back to the river from which she came.

And there,
On an urban wharf,
She leaned forward
And closed her eyes.
She smelled the mud of a continent,
And felt the current of the river
Cold inside her,
And she heard her own voice,
Low and strange,
With words that chanted from her mouth
As if she knew them from another life.

> *I am the Lady of the River*
> *the city of your dreams*
> *and I am stronger than I seem.*
> *Stay with me.*
> *Believe in me.*
> *Love me.*
> *I will be young again.*

The Author: Brod Bagert is a New Orleans trial lawyer, former City Councilman, civic activist, dreamer, loving husband and doting father, juggler, acrobat, sleight-of-hand artist, violin aficionado, and compulsive arranger of words.

The Photographer: Christopher Harris, wildman photo-lyricist of bayou and boardroom, captures images for the likes of *Time* and *Newsweek* when not otherwise occupied by the pursuit of the siren green trout of Lake Maurepas.

The photograph of former Governor John J. McKeithen on page 25 was included in this collection because it was irresistible. To conclude from its juxtaposition to *Campaign Promises* that he was a glib-talking, insincere politician before or during his tenure of office would be a mistake. John McKeithen was one of Louisiana's finest governors, and a particularly good one for the city of New Orleans.